# AFFIRMED

Thirty-five Positive Affirmations
for Every Area of Your Life

Tony Ray Smith

**Library of Congress Cataloging-in-Publication Data**

Smith, Tony Ray
Affirmed
I. Religious 2. Devotional 3. Encouragement

ISBN: 978-0-57895-945-0

DULLES PUBLISHING
C O M P A N Y
EST 2017

www.dullespublishingcompany.com

# ABOUT THE AUTHOR

Tony Ray Smith is the self-published author of four incredibly popular books including this most recent title, *Affirmed.* Tony's writing and consulting expertise encompasses the areas of personal development, leadership, productivity, and marketing as well as public and motivational speaking. He is a talented and respected leader, speaker, teacher, and personal development and business coach whose own goals embrace a sincere desire to help others achieve success.

Tony is the founder and CEO of Tony Ray Smith Enterprises, LLC which is the holding company for Catalyst Consulting and Dulles Publishing Group. The mission of Tony Ray Smith Enterprises is to help 1,000 people start to build their lives, businesses, and/or the ministries they desire by the effective setting and successful achievement of specific goals.

In addition, Tony is a duly licensed and ordained pastor and is currently the Senior Pastor of The Word Church, Inc. in Ashburn, Virginia. He has been a pastor for twelve years and an itinerant speaker for more than twenty years.

Most recently, Tony has been successfully encouraging people with the use of positive affirmations. He wants to help people learn to put specific language to affirming principles that they then need to declare in order to enhance their lives. It is his earnest desire that, by so doing, people will be encouraged to find the strength and ability to keep moving toward their dreams and their desired destinies—and that they will be walking entirely in their purpose.

# DEDICATION

This book is dedicated in loving memory of my late beloved grandmother, Beatrice Carter, whose unfailing love defined motherhood for me. At the golden age of ninety-seven, she received her wings and departed this earth on Sunday, January 13, 2019.

Beatrice, affectionately known as Bea or Ma Bea was born on Thursday, July 29, 1922 in a town called The Plains in Fauquier County, Virginia. In 1936 at the age of fourteen, she was united in Holy Matrimony to the late William Henry Carter, Sr. and they then produced seven daughters and seven sons. In addition to raising her own children, Bea was a mother to many others in the community who she helped to shape, nurture, and mold their lives.

At my formative age of six, my grandmother took on the responsibility of raising me. I am forever indebted and grateful to her because she was not only my grandmother, she was also my mother.

May Beatrice rest in peace!

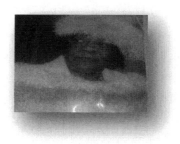

# SPECIAL THANKS

A special thanks to all the many wonderful people who support me on a daily basis. I could not do all the things I do without a great support system. First, I would like to thank my wonderful wife, Cardhia Smith, who is a devoted and supportive wife and the foundation of our family. Thanks also to my two sons, Xavier and Josiah Smith, who are the driving force to my passion. My sincere appreciation also goes to my father, Tony Ray Carter, who supports me 100 percent and beyond; and to Michele Birgans who has worked behind the scenes to encourage me. Finally, I am grateful to a wonderful church, The Word Church of Ashburn, Virginia—with one of the greatest church families a pastor could ask for.

# TABLE OF CONTENTS

# FOREWORD

In his latest book, *Affirmed*, Pastor Tony Smith offers his readers an insightful guide that teaches us how to speak life over our own lives. Oh, how I wish I had read this book many years ago when my journey of change began.

There are several definitions for affirmations but I like to define affirmations as words or phrases that give and speak life. Practicing daily positive affirmations enables us to dismantle our negative mindsets that have kept us believing we are not good enough or that we are not equipped to walk in our purpose.

As a child growing up, I believed the old phrase, "sticks and stones may break my bones but words can never hurt me." As I grew up, however, I quickly realized that the negative words spoken over my life by others, combined with those I spoke about myself, actually did hurt me. They broke my self-esteem and stifled my ability to believe I could do all things.

Our words have power! Negative words breed negativity and positive words breed positivity. Negative words spoken over our lives, whether by others or ourselves, can linger with us forever unless we break the cycle by renewing our minds.

The Word of God tells us to fix our thoughts on what is true, and honorable, and right, and pure, and lovely, and admirable. He goes on to say that we are to think about things that are excellent and worthy of praise. He tells us to fix our thoughts and to think about positive things (see Phil 4:8). Affirmations take this a step further by verbalizing our thoughts. When we speak them aloud, they become reality!

Positive affirmations have helped me renew my mind and they released me from stinking thinking, worry, and anxiety. Daily affirmations have built my confidence, aligned my heart with what God calls me—His daughter—to be, and propelled me forward so I can walk in my God-given purpose.

I am so grateful to Pastor Tony Smith for assembling this collection of positive affirmations in one book. We now no longer have to grapple with what to say and how to say it. We no longer have to search out affirmations that fit our specific circumstances. We just need to pull out this resource and speak life.

Why this book? Simple. It will change your life—but only if you allow it to! Remember—words matter. When you speak positive God-centered affirmations, you not only change your own life for the better, you also speak life over the lives of those around you.

Lady Charlet Lewis, Executive Pastor
Light of Life Church
www.ladycharlet.com

# PREFACE

Affirmations are positive declarative statements that are meant to affirm and reaffirm the speaker's possibilities, potential, and promises. As you begin to use positive affirmations, I am confident that you will soon see their benefit and that they will quickly become part of your daily routine. This practice follows a proven principle—what you put into the atmosphere will shape your reality. This not only follows a biblical law, it also adheres to a natural law which states that what you sow, you will reap. While affirmations speak to your conscious mind, they also speak to your subconscious mind—and your subconscious mind is working even when you're not deliberately thinking about a certain matter.

*Affirmed* was inspired by another book I wrote entitled *Goal For It.* At the end of *Goal For It,* I wrote some affirmations and I received dozens of great compliments about them. Many readers have been tremendously blessed and inspired by those affirmations.

This book is not intended to be read from the first page to the last page as you would read a traditional self-help guide or novel. Rather, this book was designed to serve as a resource that you can reference repeatedly. It is my prayer that *Affirmed* will provide you with specific samples of positive language that you can use in your everyday life as you strive to overcome discouragement, dismay, rejections, frustration, and desperation. *Affirmed* will serve as a resource for you by providing encouragement, some language, and a prayer starter.

*Affirmed* can also be used as a personal devotional book. I have provided inspirational quotes and scriptures to go with each affirmation. You can expand on the information I have provided by researching additional quotes and scriptures to add to each affirmation.

Finally, you can also create your own affirmations. I have written these thirty-five affirmations for you and you can use them as starting points to develop your own. I could not cover every situation for which you might need an affirmation. However, if you need an affirmation for something specific, take a look at what I've written. Hopefully, that will provide the inspiration you need to craft your own affirmations.

# INTRODUCTION

I believe Nicole Ashley said it best, "Affirmations are short, powerful, yet simple statements designed to manifest a specific goal. Positive thinking reinforced by verbal affirmations is designed to encourage a life filled with positivity and gratitude." The writer of Proverbs 18:21 stated, "Death and life are in the power of the tongue." Our words do have the power to shape our reality. Our words are guides for our actions. You cannot speak negatively and expect to get positive results. It just won't work.

These thirty-five affirmations cover the gamut of most life situations. It is sometimes hard to be positive in a negative situation or find the strength to move forward. *Affirmed* will give you the specific language you need to speak positively in every circumstance you may be facing. When trials and tribulations are present, they can often strip you of your cognitive ability to think straight. It is very common to be unable to pray while being pressured by the burdens of life. *Affirmed* enables you to continue declaring the goodness of the Lord while renouncing the plans and plots of the enemy.

As you begin to use these affirmations in your daily life, I hope they will provide you with a needed boost of strength and encouragement that enables you to continue to make steady progress through this journey called life that often seems unbearable and unfair. I like the way the Psalmist said it in Psalm 46:1. "God is our refuge and strength, an ever-present help in trouble." While these affirmations are not scriptures, I believe they were given to me by the inspiration of the Holy Spirit. Therefore, I do believe these are prophetic declarations. Prophetic declarations are bold statements based on scriptural promises that we, as believers, can use to shape our future.

My prayer for you is 3 John 2: "Beloved, I wish above all things that thou mayest prosper and be in health, even as thy soul prospereth." I further decree and declare that the Lord will grant you your heart's desires and make all your plans succeed and that the enemy's plans for your life, ministry, business, and goals will be rendered null and void.

Amen.

Tony Ray Smith

# AFFIRMED

# CHAPTER 1
# BROKENNESS

> *"Vulnerability is the birthplace of innovation, creativity, and change."*
> ~**Brene Brown**

> *"The Lord is near to the brokenhearted and saves the crushed in spirit."*
> — **Psalm 34:18**

# Breaking Brokenness

Brokenness is a temporary state and not my permanent situation.

I refuse to make life-changing decisions during moments of brokenness.

I will not allow my brokenness to break me, emotionally bankrupt me, or make me bitter.

My brokenness did not catch God by surprise, so there is a plan.

Therefore, I resolve that:

I will use my brokenness as a tool to minister to others.

I can make it on broken pieces.

Broken, bruised, and battered is my current reality but not my finality.

Yes, this is a part of my biography, but it will not be printed in my obituary.

I have been broken, but I will be better!

I am exchanging brokenness for a blessing.

# CHAPTER 2
# CHILDREN

*"Your greatest legacy will not be your career accomplishments, the church you built, or your educational achievements but it will be your children (Xavier and Josiah)."*
— **Rev. Dr. Randy M. Haynes to Pastor Tony Smith**

*"Children are a heritage from the LORD, offspring a reward from him."*
— **Psalm 127:3**

# The Children's Blessing

My children are blessed.

My children walk in supernatural favor.

My children are protected by the blood of Jesus.

My children are graced to accomplish their God-given purpose.

My children are thoughtful, kind, and giving; living out the fruit of the spirit (Galatian 5:22).

My children will not be consumers only but will make differences in the world that impact the lives of many.

My children lack no good thing.

My children will not be depressed, despondent, or destitute.

My children will not suffer from mental illnesses.

Children will be led, guided, and directed by the Holy Spirit all the days of their lives. They will have a sensitivity to hear his voice and movement in their lives.

I secure their future now with all the good things God has for them, and I pray above all things that their souls will prosper naturally and spiritually.
— Selah

# CHAPTER 3
# CONFIDENCE

*"It is not who you think you are that is holding you back; it is who you think you are not that keeps holding you back."*
— **Dr. Keith Johnson**

*"For I am confident of this very thing, that He who began a good work in you will perfect it until the day of Christ Jesus."*
— **Philippians 1:6**

# Confidence Confirmed

Before the foundation of the world;
God knew me.

I am handcrafted by the God of the universe.

I am fearfully and wonderfully made.

I have everything I need at this moment to accomplish
what needs to be accomplished now.

Nothing missing and nothing broken.

I am who I am by the grace of God.

I will walk in the divine purpose of God for my life.

I do not have to bow to pressure to become
someone else.

I am confident in my God-given ability.

I am confident in my God-given assignment.

I am confident in my God-given authority.

No one can beat me at being who God made me to be.

# CHAPTER 4
# CREATIVITY

*"Creativity is not a feeling; it is a discipline."*
—**Tommy Tenney**

*"... and he (God) has filled him (you) with the Spirit of God with skill, with intelligence, with knowledge, and with all craftsmanship to devise artistic designs, to work in gold and silver and bronze, in cutting stones for settings, and in carving wood for work in every skilled craft."*
— **Exodus 5:30 - 33**

# Creativity Come Forth

Because the ultimate creator lives in me, I am creative.

Therefore, I awaken the creative genius which is me.

I can create from an idea from God, a desire to cause it to manifest, and the discipline to make it work.

God has given me original plans, witty inventions, and creative thoughts.

I am creative.

The world is waiting on my creativeness.

I recognize and dismiss all creativity blockers—doubt, fear, procrastination, distractions, and apathy.

I am a creative person.

I will create.

I must create.

Today, I create.

# CHAPTER 5
# DEBT

*"The rich rule over the poor, and the borrower is slave to the lender."*
— **King David**

*"Owe no man anything but to love one another, for he that loveth another hath fulfilled the law."*
— **Romans 13:8**

# Deliverance from Debt

I am debt free.

I am disciplined with my finances.

I practice delayed gratification.

I spend cautiously;
Sow generously;
Lend wisely.

I break the cycle of debt.

I reject the mentality of poverty.

I release the discipline to save, the wisdom to manage my finances responsibly, and the opportunity to be free from the slavery of debt.

Death to debt!

# CHAPTER 6
# DELIVERANCE

*"Sin will take you further than you want to go and keep you longer than you want to stay."*
— **Minister Muriel Swanson**

*"Stay Free"*
— **Pastor Rene Hudnull**

*"It is for freedom that Christ has set us free. Stand firm, then, and do not let yourselves be burdened again by a yoke of slavery."*
— **Galatians 5:1**

# Deliverance Delivered

I make a decision to be delivered.

I reject past and present soul ties.

I close all open doors and gates that lead to sin.

I choose to be free.

Jesus died that I might be free.

I walk in my God-given and divine freedom.

I lay myself on the spiritual surgical table so that God may perform surgery on me and remove anything that is not like him.

This stops with me and will not be passed down my generational line.

I am delivered. No longer bound. No more chains holding me.

Thank you, Jesus, for freedom in and of you!

# CHAPTER 7
# DISCOURAGEMENT

*"When discouragement comes, don't stop. Dig deep and fight it through!"*
— **T.B. Joshua**

*"Have I not commanded you? Be strong and courageous. Do not be frightened, and do not be dismayed, for the Lord your God is with you wherever you go."*
— **Joshua 1:9**

# Disarming Discouragement

Discouragement is a tool of delay from the devil.

Discouragement can only go as far as I allow it to go. I cannot stop it from coming, but I can stop it from staying.

I will not be discouraged.

I will not allow discouragement to delay my destiny, detour my dreams, or arrest my development.

I destroy the power of discouragement and release the overcomer within me.

I will not allow discouragement to become a stronghold.

The devil is a liar.

I am encouraged.

I am victorious.

I am a conqueror.

Watch me win!

# CHAPTER 8
# FAITH

*"Darkness, despair, disruption, and delay are often the activators of great faith."*
— **Tony Ray Smith**

*"6: But without faith it is impossible to please him: for he that cometh to God must believe that he is, and that he is a rewarder of them that diligently seek him."*
— **Hebrews 11:6**

# Faith Forward

I will not allow my feelings to override my faith.

I will not allow my frustrations to abort my faith.

I walk by faith.

I speak by faith.

I believe by faith.

I see through the lens of faith.

I am expecting great things in my life by faith and, most importantly, I live by faith.


Faith Note: It is important to realize that there is a fine line between faith and foolishness. However, as you walk out your faith, remember that faith is preceded by a Word from God.

# CHAPTER 9
# FAMILY

> *"A family tie is like a tree; it can bend but it cannot break."*
> — **African proverb**

> *"15: But if serving the Lord seems undesirable to you, then choose for yourselves this day whom you will serve, whether the gods your ancestors served beyond the Euphrates, or the gods of the Amorites, in whose land you are living. But as for me and my household, we will serve the Lord."*
> — **Joshua 24:15**

# Fortifying Family

My family has a future in God.

No generation will arise that doesn't know
the God of Abraham, Isaac, and Jacob.

I renounce negative generational recurrences in the family.

I cancel diabolic schemes planned for my family.

I declare generational blessings on my family.

I decree uncommon favors for my family.

I release supernatural provision over my family.

I pray divine protection from danger, both seen and
unseen.

I secure our sons and daughters of my family's future.

We all walk in the Abrahamic blessing.
(See Abrahamic Blessing – page 80)

No weapon formed against my family shall prosper. It is
so. In Jesus' name. Amen.

# CHAPTER 10
# FEAR

*"Always do what you are afraid to do."*
— **Ralph Waldo Emerson.**

*"The Lord is with me; I will not be afraid. What can mere mortals do to me?"*
— **Psalm 118:16**

# Fighting Fear

I will not fear.

I have no reason to fear.

So what, if I fail; at least I tried.

I will not be paralyzed by the realness that I feel of fear.

I fear no man. I fear no task.
I will do it unafraid. I will face it unafraid.
And, I will accomplish it unafraid.

I will accomplish it even if afraid because
success lies on the other side of my fear.

Impact lies on the other side of this fear.

I command fear to dissolve and faith to rise.

Jude 24: Now unto him that is able to keep you from
falling, and to present you faultless before the presence of
his glory with exceeding joy. 25: To the only wise God our
Savior, be glory and majesty, dominion, and power both
now and ever. Amen.

# CHAPTER 11
# FINANCES

> *"If a person gets his attitude toward money straight, it will help straighten out almost every other area in his life."*
> — **Rev. Billy Graham, Evangelist**

> *"And my God will supply every need of yours according to his riches in glory in Christ Jesus."*
> — **Philippians 4:19**

# Fixing Finances

I walk in financial freedom.

I make wise choices with my finances.

I exercise discipline with my money.

I do not buy impulsively.

I use Godly wisdom to manage my finances.

God is my source.

Giving is essential.

Generosity is a lifestyle.

I reject poverty.

I receive wealth.

I honor God with my finances.

I am a channel that God uses to bless others.

# CHAPTER 12
# FORGIVENESS

*"Forgiveness is giving up the hope that the past could be any different."*
— **Oprah Winfrey**

*And whenever you stand praying, forgive, if you have anything against anyone, so that your Father also who is in heaven may forgive you your trespasses."*
— **Mark 11:25**

# Finding Forgiveness

I am forgiven; therefore I forgive.

I give myself the gift of forgiveness and
I extend that gift to others.

I walk in forgiveness.

I confess forgiveness.

I stand in forgiveness.

I reject anger, bitterness, and resentment.

I reject the burden of unforgiveness and
I release the joy, freedom, and miracles that come
with forgiveness.

I command the blessings of the Lord to be manifest
so that others are released with forgiveness.

I choose forgiveness.

It is so.

# CHAPTER 13
## GOALS

> *"Discipline is the bridge between goals and accomplishment."*
> — **Jim Rohn**

> *"The plans of the diligent lead to profit as surely as haste leads to poverty."*
> — **Proverbs 21:5**

# Goal For It

I refuse to stay in the place of mediocrity.
Therefore, I set goals.

I will establish plans as a path to pursue my goals.

I do not wait for inspiration.

I am driven, determined, and disciplined.

I reject laziness, negativity, and limiting beliefs.

I release endurance, power, and energy to
make my goals a reality.

I do not waste time on activities that do not
aid me in my pursuit of realizing my goals.

I am making an investment now in my future.

I will not be distracted, delayed, or denied.

I will reach my God-given goals.

# CHAPTER 14
# GRIEF

> *"Grief is the price we pay for love."*
> —**Queen Elizabeth II**

> *"He heals the brokenhearted and bandages their wounds."*
> — **Psalm 147:3**

# Grappling with Grief

I acknowledge that I am grieving.

The pain and the feelings I feel are real.

Grief is normal.
It is not weakness or
a lack of faith.

I will not suppress or ignore my grief and
act like things are OK to make others feel comfortable.

I will be intentional about dealing with grief.

Grief is manageable and
I will manage it and not allow it to manage me.

I will not allow the enemy to turn my grief
into depression, despair, or destitution.

I pray that God, the source of MY hope,
will fill me completely with joy and peace because I trust in
him.

I release the overflow of peace and consolation with
confident hope through the power of the Holy Spirit.

Amen.

# CHAPTER 15
# HAPPINESS

*"The key to being happy is knowing you have the power to choose what to accept and what to let go."*
— **Dodinsky**

*"I'm Happy in Jesus"*
— **Carolyn "Peewee" Carter**
*(My Deceased Aunt)*

*"He who heeds the word wisely will find good, and whoever trusts in the Lord, happy is he."*
— **Proverbs 16:20**

# Because I'm Happy

I make a conscious decision, choice, and plan
to be happy.

I refuse to allow my situation to determine my mood.

I reject tying my happiness to the decisions of other people.

I renounce the plans of the enemy to bring me desolation
and despair.

I release the oil of gladness,
the aroma of serenity,
the spirit of joy,
the atmosphere of peace, and
the victory over defeat.

I am happy because I am his (Jesus).

# CHAPTER 16
# HEALTH

> *"It is health that is the real wealth, and not pieces of gold and silver."*
> — **Mahatma Gandhi**

> *"Beloved, I pray that all may go well with you and that you may be in good health, as it goes well with your soul."*
> — **3 John 2:1**

# Health Quintupled

My health is my wealth.

I acknowledge that health is multidimensional,
physical, emotional, mental, relational, and spiritual.
Therefore,
I will endeavor to maintain my health
with various forms of self-care.

I will make healthier food selections.

I will engage in some form of physical activity daily.

I will practice self-awareness.

I will take time for myself.

I will learn something new to expand my knowledge every
day.

I will build relationships that positively affect my health.

I will take time for spiritual disciplines such as
prayer, worship, study, and meditation on the Word of
God.

I will make daily choices that allow me to be whole and
healthy.

It will not be easy, but it will be worth it.

# CHAPTER 17
# HURT

> *"In the end, some of your greatest pain becomes your greatest strength."*
> — **Drew Barrymore**

> *"I have told you these things, so that in Me you may have peace. In this world you will have trouble. But take heart! I have overcome the world."*
> —**John 16:33**

# Emancipation from Hurt

I am hurt because I care.

I am hurt but I have hope.

I am hurt but
I will not allow this hurt to become
the seed of hostility and animosity.

I will not allow this hurt to poison
future relationships and opportunities.

I will learn the lesson that hurt teaches.

I embrace the possibilities that lie
in the shadows of hurt.

I will allow God to heal me from hurt.

I release the people who hurt me.

I thank God for the freedom to walk in the healing from
hurt.

I am an overcomer.

# CHAPTER 18
## I AM STATEMENTS

*"I am who I am. Not who you think I am. Not who you want me to be. I am me."*
— **Brigitte Nicole**

*"For we are God's handiwork, created in Christ Jesus to do good works, which God prepared in advance for us to do."*
— **Ephesians 2:10**

# I Am

I was made in the image and likeness of I Am. Therefore, I am.

I am courageous.

I am creative.

I am an overcomer.

I am a victor.

I am righteous.

I am fearfully and wonderfully made.

I am complete.

I am confident.

I am unique.

I am blessed.

I am wealthy.

I am enough.

# CHAPTER 19
## IDENTITY IN CHRIST

*"God is always revealing your identity and purpose."*
— **Dr. Randy M. Haynes**

*"Therefore, if anyone is in Christ, he is a new creation.
The old has passed away; behold, the new has come."*
— **2 Corinthians 5:17**

# Identity Revealed

My identity is found in no one and nothing but Christ.

I am in a new creation. Therefore, I no longer identify with my old self and old ways.

I am a part of the royal family.

I am a child of God.

I am no longer a servant, but a friend of God.

I am an heir and joint heir to the King of Kings.

I am no longer bound.

I abide in him and him in me.

God is my father.
Jesus is my big brother and
the Holy Spirit is my guide.

I am complete in him!

# CHAPTER 20
## JOY

> *"We cannot cure the world of sorrows, but we can choose to live in joy."*
> — **Joseph Campbell**

> *"May the God of hope fill you with all joy and peace in believing, so that by the power of the Holy Spirit you may abound in hope."*
> — **Romans 15:13**

# I Choose Joy

The joy of the Lord is my strength.

My joy is replenished from the depths of
the spirit of God.

I ignite the springs of joy to overflow in my life
and into the lives of others.

I am a source of joy for others.

No one will come in contact with me and remain the same
or sad.

I will rejoice and be glad.

I choose to rejoice and be joyful.

I change atmospheres of depression or despair
and charge them with joy.

Even in bad news situations or circumstances,
I choose joy!

I decree the fruit of the spirit of joy to be alive, active, and
abundant in my life and in the lives of those around me.

# CHAPTER 21
# LETTING GO

*"Some of us think holding on makes us strong; but sometimes it is letting go."*
— **Hermann Hesse**

*"6 ... a time to search and a time to give up, a time to keep and a time to throw away,"*
— **Ecclesiastes 3:6**

# Let It Go

It's OK to let go.

I am not weak for letting go.

I will not be embarrassed for letting go.

It's just simply time for me to let go.

I will let go of that which is no longer good for me.

I will let go of that which no longer serves me in this season.

I will not be manipulated by others for letting go.

I am not a bad person because I have chosen to let go.

I must let go of that to which I am holding onto if it is harming me.

I'm letting go so that God can do a new thing in me, for me, and around me.

# CHAPTER 22
## LOVE

*"Love recognizes no barriers. It jumps hurdles, leaps fences, penetrates walls to arrive at its destination full of hope."*
— **Maya Angelou**

*"37: Jesus replied: 'Love the Lord your God with all your heart and with all your soul and with all your mind.[a] 38: This is the first and greatest commandment. 39: And the second is like it: Love your neighbor as yourself.'[b] 40: All the Law and the Prophets hang on these two commandments."*
— **Matthew 22:37-40**

# Embracing Love

God is love; therefore,
I choose to love.

I will love in spite of
disappointment, betrayal, or abandonment.

I reject hate, bitterness, and anger.
These I refuse to carry in my
spirit, mind, or soul.

My actions will be guided by love.

My speech will be directed by love.

My attitude will be regulated by love.

I release those who have hurt me, misused me, or
rejected me because of love.

I am loved by God. Therefore, I love others
like God loves me.

# CHAPTER 23
## LOW SELF-ESTEEM

> *"It's not what you are that is holding you back. It's what you think you are not."*
> — **Denis Waitley**

> *"Look at the birds of the air: they neither sow nor reap nor gather into barns, and yet your heavenly Father feeds them. Are you not of more value than they?"*
> — **Matthew 6:26**

# Low Self-esteem Rejected

My value doesn't come from within or without, but from
him.

I embrace me,
all of me—
flaws, shortcomings, and weaknesses—
they all make up me.

No one can beat me at being me because
there is only one of me and there
will never be another me.

I love me.

I will not pretend to be another,
or hide my authentic self, or
dumb down me to make others
feel comfortable.

I fully embrace the me God made me to be.

# CHAPTER 24
# MARRIAGE

> *"A good marriage isn't something you find, it's something you make, and you have to keep on making it."*
> — **Author Unknown**

> *"Let marriage be held in honor among all..."*
> —**Hebrews 13:4**

# My Marriage Matters

I am not perfect. Therefore,
I ascribe no perfection mandate for my spouse.

I allow my spouse room for grace to grow into the person
they are meant to be.

I reject the thoughts of divorce.

There is no Plan B.

I renounce all former and present soul ties.

I reject the interjections of the devil.

I affirm what God has made others to be.

We do not compete with each other, but
we complete one another. This means
that we embrace each other's differences.

We have a happy marriage.

We have an impactful marriage.

God has joined us together. Nothing but death
can separate us.

# CHAPTER 25
# MIND

*"You have power over your mind, not outside events. Realize this, and you will find strength."*
— **Marcus Aurelius**

*… "for, Who has known the mind of the Lord so as to instruct him? But we have the mind of Christ."*
— **1 Corinthians 2:16**

# Minding My Mind

I have the mind of Christ.

My mind is strong, alert, and active.

My mind is receptive to new ideas, thoughts, and changes.

I reject negativity, doubt, and fear.

I give the devil no permission, space, or place in my mind.

I defuse every trick, plot, and scheme the enemy has
designed for my mind.

I will not lose my mind.
I will expand my mind by reading and learning.

I give my mind permission to think new thoughts,
dream new dreams, and give birth
to new visions.

I am not a limited thinker.

I release my mind to think forward,
to think creatively, and to think expansively.

# CHAPTER 26
## OVERWHELMED

*"You must tell yourself, No matter how hard it is, or how hard it gets, I'm going to make it."*
— **Les Brown**

*"Come to me, all of you who are weary and carry heavy burdens, and I will give you rest."*
— **Matthew 11:28**

# Overcoming Overwhelmed

Overwhelmed is a moment.

What I am dealing with will pass.

A brighter day is ahead of me.

I will not make any major decisions at this moment.

I will trust God.

I will exercise faith.

I will be OK.

I will not quit.

I will not give up.

I will try again another day.

God is on my side.

Grace and mercy are following me.

I am determined to overcome being overwhelmed.
I have victory over it and not it over me.

# CHAPTER 27
## PAST

> "The past is a good reference, but a terrible residence."
> — **Tony Ray Smith**

> "Forget the former things; do not dwell on the past."
> — **Isaiah 43:18**

> "Once again you will have compassion on us. You will trample our sins under your feet and throw them into the depths of the ocean!"
> —**Micah 7:19**

# Moving On!

I will not allow the pain of my past to paralyze my future.

My past has no power in my present.

My past does not nullify the promise and purpose in my life.

I am no longer shackled to my past.

I am more than my past mistakes.

I silence the deadly whispers of my past.

I am moving forward beyond my past and into my promise.

# CHAPTER 28
# PEACE

> *"Do not let the behavior of others destroy your inner peace."*
> — **Dalai Lama**

> *"Peace I leave with you; my peace I give to you. Not as the world gives do I give to you. Let not your hearts be troubled, neither let them be afraid."*
> — **John 14:27**

# Unexplainable Peace

I will live in peace, at peace, and with peace.

I dwell in a peace that passes all understanding.

I will not allow people or situations to disrupt, detain, or destroy my peace.

There is no separation between me and peace.
Therefore, there will be peace in my home, peace on my job, and peace everywhere I am.

I shift hostile environments because
my presence brings
peace.

I know the author of peace.

Peace overflows in my life. Therefore, I share peace with everyone I encounter.

Shalom.

# CHAPTER 29
# PURPOSE

*"Purpose is revealed in prayer."*
— **Pastor Tony Ray Smith**

*"The Lord will fulfill His purpose in me..."*
—**Psalm 138:8**

# Purposely Purposeful

I will live in and on purpose.

I will thrive in my purpose.

I will fulfill my God-given purpose.

I will not abort my purpose because of pressure, pain, or persecution.

People are depending on me to live out my purpose.

Problems will not deter me from my purpose.

I declare to walk in my purpose every day.

I've been purposely positioned to prosper in my purpose.

# CHAPTER 30
# SINGLENESS

*"Being single doesn't make you weak. It means that you are strong enough to be on your own."*
— **Xavier Zayas**

*"I wish that all of you were as I am. But each of you has your own gift from God; one has this gift, another has that. Now to the unmarried and the widows I say: It is good for them to stay unmarried, as I do."*
— **1 Corinthians 7:7-8**

# Winning Single

There is nothing wrong with me because I am single.

My singleness is not a curse.

My singleness is not a problem to be solved.

My singleness is not weakness.

I am whole. Nothing is broken
and nothing is missing.

I am not miserable and waiting.

I will enjoy my singleness.

I reject any societal pressure to be married just to be
married.

I reject loneliness.

I will not be manipulated into relationships that
will not go anywhere.

I am determined to grow, and go, and glow in my
singleness.

I'm living my best life now.

# CHAPTER 31
# SPEAKING

> *"Words have creative power and can create happiness or sadness, good or bad, or dreams with the potential to be destroyed."*
> — **Tony Ray Smith**

> *"Let the words of my mouth and the meditation of my heart be acceptable in Your sight, O Lord, my rock and my Redeemer."*
> — **Psalm 19:14**

# Speaking Affirmation

written by Michael Hyatt

I am not here by accident. God sent me. To these people.
At exactly this time.
That's because He has a purpose; therefore, I have a
purpose in being here.

What I have to share today is vitally important. It matters.
To them, to their loved ones, and to all the people they will
eventually impact.

Those who hear this message will be changed forever.
Years from now, they will look back on today and say, "It
all started there."

Through Christ, I can do all things. He has given me every
resource I need to succeed.

I have the energy, the passion, and the message to make a
huge impact—now and for eternity.

By God's grace, I am prepared. My heart and spirit are wide
open. I will connect and see transformation.

# CHAPTER 32
# STRENGTH

*"A hero is an ordinary individual who finds the strength to persevere and endure in spite of overwhelming obstacles."*
— **Christopher Reeve**

*"In the day when I cried out, You answered me, And made me bold with strength in my soul."*
— **Psalm 138:3**

# Strength to Strength

I am stronger than I think I am.

I can endure tribulation.

I can withstand the storms of life.

I will not depend on my own strength because it is finite.

My strength comes from God—the Heavenly Father.

I will not bow to the external pressure that I feel although
it is real.

I will remain steadfast, unmovable, and unshakable.

I will emerge stronger, wiser, and better.

I am strengthened.

I will survive.

I'm on my way to thriving.

# CHAPTER 33
## WEALTH

*"Wealth is a mindset; not a number on a balance sheet."*
— **Pastor Tony Ray Smith**

*"9: Honor the Lord with your wealth, with the first fruits of all your crops; 10: then your barns will be filled to overflowing, and your vats will brim over with new wine."*
— **Proverbs 3:9-10**

# Walking in Wealth

I will honor the Lord first with my wealth in time, talent, and treasure.

All my needs are met.

I lack nothing financially, spiritually, or emotionally.

I walk in the abundant favor of God.

I reject the poverty mindset.

I embrace a wealth mindset.

I release the blessings of the Lord. For it is he who gives me the power to get wealth.

I am a lender, not a borrower.

I owe no man anything but to love them.

I manage wealth. Wealth doesn't manage me.

I am wealthy and it is a blessing.

I am a conduit to be used by God to flow blessings freely and generously.

# CHAPTER 34
# WRITING

*"Start writing, no matter what. The water does not flow until the faucet is turned on."*
— **Louis L'Amour**

*"Thus says the Lord, the God of Israel,*
*'Write all the words which I have spoken to you in a book.'"*
— **Jeremiah 30:2**

# A Writer's Affirmation

I can write. I have the expertise, knowledge, and experience
to produce high quality content
in a relatively short amount of time.

I am focused. I am alert. My mind is open to receive
direction and redirection
from the Holy Spirit.

I will produce clear, concrete, and concise content that will
impact those who will read it
and it will add value to their lives.

By God's grace and his power, his will can be done through
me.

# CHAPTER 35
## CLOSURE

> *"Sometimes you get closure, sometimes you don't. You just have to walk away knowing you tried your best, and let God handle the rest."*
> — **Author Unknown**

> *"And we know that in all things God works for the good of those who love him, who[a] have been called according to his purpose."*
> — **Romans 8:28**

# Closing Chapters

Everything is not meant to be.

Some things and some people are only for a brief season.

I will not get stuck in a moment.

I must continue on.

I will not put a comma where God has ordained a period.

I accept the fact that I may never get
the closure that I want but I
embrace the closure that I need.

Now...

God, grant me the serenity to accept the things I cannot
change,
courage to change the things I can,
and wisdom to know the difference.
(~Serenity Prayer)

10: And after you have suffered for a little while, the God
of all grace, who has called you to His eternal glory in
Christ, will Himself restore you, secure you, strengthen you,
and establish you. 11: To Him be the power forever and
ever. Amen
(1 Peter 5:10-11)

# BONUS
# BEDTIME

> "God can do more in your sleep than you can do in your work."
> **– Pastor Tony Ray Smith**

> "In vain you rise early and stay up late, toiling for food to eat for he grants sleep to those he loves."
> **— Psalm 127:2**

# Go To Sleep

Everyone is tired when they wake up. When the alarm goes off, I will get up and get going.

I will be alert and full of energy.

I will wake up refreshed and ready to impact someone's life positively.

I release from my mind and spirit all projects and tasks that were not completed today.

I release myself from all negative energy, thoughts, and feelings.

Because of God's grace, I will wake up tomorrow to see another day and will be productive in it for the glorification of God and the edification of others.

# The Abrahamic Blessing

"I will make you into a great nation,
and I will bless you;
I will make your name great,
and you will be a blessing.
I will bless those who bless you,
and whoever curses you I will curse;
and all peoples on earth
will be blessed through you."

~ **Genesis 12:1-2**

# CONNECT WITH TONY

To obtain more information, visit his websites:
www.tonyraysmith.com
www.goalforitnow.com
www.youcanwriteabook.com

Facebook Page
www.facebook.com/iamtonyraysmith

Twitter:
**Iamtonyraysmith**

Instagram
**Iamtonyraysmith**

LinkedIn
**Tonyraysmith**

Sign up for Tony's newsletter and blog post at:
www.tonyraysmith.com/email

Made in the USA
Middletown, DE
02 October 2023

39960387R00051